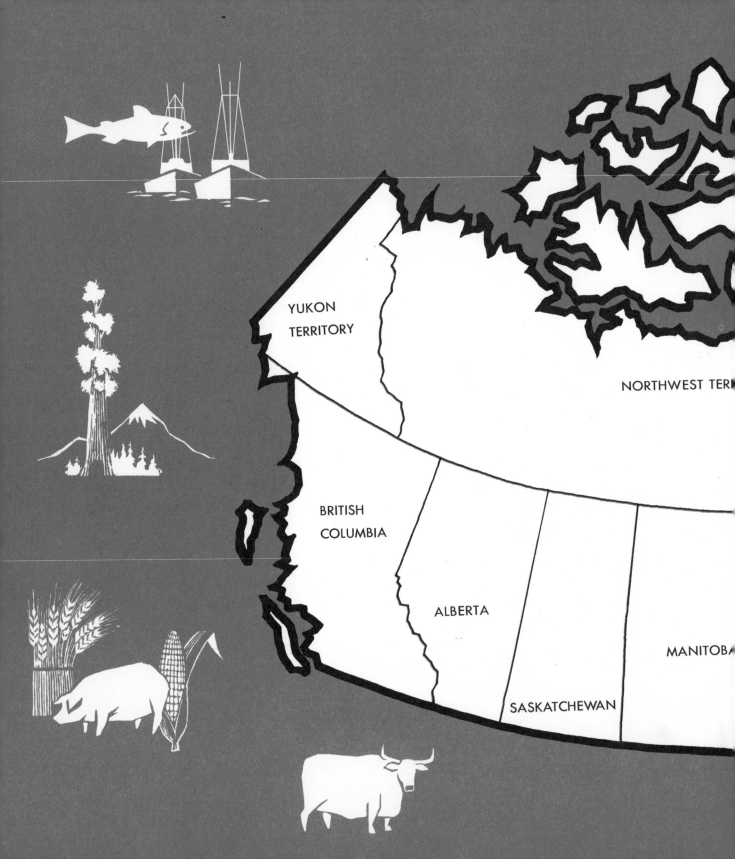

YUKON
TERRITORY

NORTHWEST TER

BRITISH
COLUMBIA

ALBERTA

SASKATCHEWAN

MANITOBA

TORIES

HUDSON
BAY

NEWFOUNDLAND

QUEBEC

ONTARIO

GULF OF ST. LAWRENCE

P. E. I.

NOVA SCOTIA

NEW
BRUNSWICK

Enchantment of America

CANADA

By Dorothy Wood

Illustrations by Harvey Shelton

CHILDRENS PRESS, Chicago

The author is grateful for
the fine consultant help of
William J. Nelson
who is on the staff of the
Teachers' College in Stratford, Ontario.

Contents

The land

Canada Is a Giant

Canada is a giant of a country that occupies most of the northern part of North America. It reaches from the ice-capped polar regions as far south as Detroit and Buffalo in the United States, about 3,000 miles, and from the Pacific Ocean to far east of the United States' Atlantic coastline—nearly 4,000 miles. A plane traveling from New York City to London, England, has covered a third of the distance when it crosses Canada's Newfoundland and heads out over the Atlantic. The eastern city of St. John's in Newfoundland is much nearer London than it is to Vancouver, on Canada's west coast.

Canada has ten provinces, besides territories that occupy its far north. The Atlantic Provinces are Newfoundland, Nova Scotia, New Brunswick, and Prince Edward Island. Newfoundland's big neighbor, the province of Quebec, has many hundreds of miles of shoreline on Atlantic waters, as well as on big Hudson Bay. Southeast Quebec fronts on the Gulf of St. Lawrence, and the St. Lawrence River slices through this southeast side, leaving some of the province south of the river. This part is the famed Gaspé Peninsula.

West of Quebec and running north around Hudson Bay is the broad province of Ontario. To the south, Ontario fronts on every one of the Great Lakes except Lake Michigan. This big province sprawls so far from east to west that it lies north of the states of New York, Pennsylvania, Ohio, Michigan, Wisconsin, and Minnesota—a province as wide as the United States' Middle West, with some of her East thrown in!

9

West of Ontario are the three Prairie Provinces, Manitoba, bordering Hudson Bay on the northeast, and Saskatchewan and Alberta. In western Alberta the land rises to the Rocky Mountains, and its western neighbor, British Columbia, is a province of both rugged mountains and Pacific seacoast.

North of all these are the territories of Canada. Yukon Territory lies directly north of British Columbia and is the eastern neighbor of Alaska. East of Yukon and north of the provinces, all the land is called the Northwest Territories—truly, the "top of the world." Much of this land reaches far north of the Arctic Circle and is broken up into huge islands, washed by Baffin Bay on the east and by the Arctic Ocean on the north and west. Only the north of Greenland is nearer the North Pole than the tip of Canada's Ellesmere Island.

Wilderness Is King

Most of Canada's people (nine-tenths of about 18,000,000 people) live within 200 miles of the United States border. Here are the big cities, the industries, the farms and ranches, the fisheries, many of the mines. Farther north, settlement becomes more and more scattered.

Why is most of Canada virtually unsettled? The countries of Norway, Sweden, and Finland are much farther north than the big cities of Canada, and so are many of the great cities of Europe. So the encroaching north is only part of the reason why Canada's people cling to its southern border.

There are three great wilderness areas in Canada that have been almost proof against wide-spread human settlement. These are the frozen Arctic region of the north; the broad north-south band of rugged Rocky Mountains and other mountains in the west, called the Cordilleran System, and the Canadian Shield. These three great areas are Canada's frontier. They are in sharp contrast to other geographical regions of Canada: the fertile agricultual lands and fishing grounds of the Atlantic provinces; the rich lowlands of the St. Lawrence and the Great Lakes; the interior plains that lie between the Shield and the mountains, with the broad, flat, and fertile prairies in their southern half; and the wet, almost subtropical Pacific Coast.

The Canadian Shield

The Canadian Shield (also called the Laurentian Shield) covers nearly half of Canada. It reaches westward from Newfoundland and Baffin Island, surrounds Hudson Bay, and covers most of Manitoba, the northern half of Saskatchewan, and most of the Northwest Territories. Through all of this land, the Shield is a forbidding, solid foundation of rock, most of it granite. Hard and bare, it often forms the surface itself; or it is thinly overlaid with water in thousands of lakes, big and little; or with swamps, called muskegs; or with rocky soil piled up in low hills. Thousands of square miles of it are deeply forested; other thousands lie north of the limit of trees, where the quick-growing plants of the tundra are the only vegetation.

More than two billion years ago, great pressures within the earth pushed the land upward. High mountains were formed. Over vast areas, molten rock lay underground, and gradually it cooled and hardened—a high "bedrock" or earth's "basement"; a solid shield of rock that has never to this day been broken up by mountain-building pressures from within or erosion from without. Gradually the early mountains wore away and earth from them was carried by streams and spread across the rock foundation. South and west of the Shield, shallow seas came up and covered some of the land. But the Shield was higher than the lands around it, and most of it stood higher than the water and was not changed by it.

Ice on the Shield

In more recent times—between one and two million years ago—another kind of change came to North America. Ice took over about three-fourths of it. In this northern three-quarters, great sheets of ice several thousand feet thick covered nearly all the land from one ocean to another. Pushed by their own weight, these continental glaciers moved down toward the oceans in the east and west, and southward through the center of the continent. Grinding along under tremendous weight, they scoured off the soil and loose rock that lay on the Canadian Shield and carried these materials along, depositing them as rich soil in the Middle West of the United States. The bedrock of the Shield was left bare, and, as we have seen, it is still only sparsely covered. In many spots that rise bare to the surface, we can see the deep ruts and scratches made by the ice sheets as they moved over it.

Much of the land sank under the tremendous weight of the glaciers, especially a vast basin in the middle of the Shield. This great depression filled with melt-water and became the 500-mile-wide Hudson Bay.

To the south and west the melting ice dropped moraines, or hills, of earth and rock, blocking the natural drainage of the water, and so the Great Lakes were formed; Lake Winnipeg, Great Slave Lake, and Great Bear Lake are others in this chain that was formed along the edge of the Shield when the vast ice sheets melted.

At least four times the ice sheets formed and moved down across the land—then melted in a warmer period—then formed again. The last big melting started about 25,000 years ago and continued until, about 10,000 years ago, most of the ice sheets disappeared. The ice cap that still covers Greenland, 6,000 to more than 11,000 feet thick, is all that remains of them.

The Land Today

The ice left the land much as it is today. The million-and-a-half square miles of the Shield are largely wilderness, peppered with thousands of lakes and slashed by uncounted rivers. The thin, rocky soil is unsuitable for agriculture, and the solid-rock foundation is unfriendly

12

to the building of roads that must come with settlement. Yet here is a rich storehouse of treasure: great deposits of valuable minerals; far-flung forests—the famous Canadian "bush"—that thrive wherever roots can find soil to cling to; tremendous water power from rivers that fall swiftly seaward from the rocky highlands—rivers such as the Ottawa and Saguenay in Quebec and the Hamilton in Labrador. All along the southern fringe of this huge storehouse, Canadians have made their homes and built their cities. More and more, they are reaching into it and making use of its treasure.

13

The Atlantic Region

Southeast of the Shield, where the land juts into the Atlantic Ocean, the Appalachian Mountains rose and continued to rise southwestward through the continent. The Appalachians are the oldest mountains in North America. They started rising more than two hundred million years ago.

In Canada they, too, and the Atlantic seaboard were covered by ice sheets. Here the land sank under the weight of ice. Then as the ice melted and more and more water poured into the oceans, the level of the ocean rose and "drowned" the coastlands. Water came up over the edge of the continent, flowing into the mouths of rivers and up the valleys between the mountains—into all the low spots—and flooded them.

So today we have the Gulf of St. Lawrence at the mouth of the St. Lawrence River, as well as hundreds of islands, peninsulas, gulfs, bays, and straits all along the coast. We have the broad "continental shelf" that extends far out into the ocean. It is the old, drowned border of the continent. Here are the famous fishing "banks" such as the Grand Banks off Newfoundland. The depth of the water may drop from less than 100 feet on the banks to 10,000 feet and more just off the shelf.

We have, too, the Appalachian mountain lands that were too high to be drowned, and that today are the highlands of hilly Newfoundland Island, Nova Scotia, and New Brunswick. Here, then, at the edge of the Atlantic and perhaps extending far into it, is the northern terminal on North America of the great system of Appalachian Mountains.

15

St. Lawrence Lowlands

A great lowland blessed with rich soil lies along the St. Lawrence River. Its queen city, Montreal, is 800 miles upriver from the sea, yet is only 58 feet above sea level. Extending still farther westward, the lowlands form a peninsula between Lakes Ontario, Erie, and Huron. But the altitude rises gradually here, and with it the water level of the Great Lakes, until the water of Lake Superior lies 580 feet above Montreal.

Water drains into the Great Lakes from all directions. On the Canadian side, it drains rapidly. Here, all along the borders of the Canadian Shield, the land rose as the ice melted, and it dumps its water swiftly into the lakes south of it. Almost all this water drains from Lake Superior and the other Great Lakes into the St. Lawrence River. Sometimes it falls rapidly over sudden drops in the land, as it does in St. Mary's River between Lake Superior and Lake Huron; and in Niagara Falls, between Lake Erie and Lake Ontario.

All this water drains through a lowland that was penetrated deeply by the sea when the early coastline was drowned. So here, in the St. Lawrence River, is a giant junction of fresh water and salt water. Quebec, hundreds of miles inland, still has the sea's salt-water tides in her harbor.

The Interior Plains

Canada's Interior Plains are the northern portion of a vast interior lowland that occupies the center of the North American continent, reaching across the United States from the Rocky Mountains to the Appalachians. Canada's plains lie between the Shield and the Rockies. They go northward from the United States border in a 700-mile-wide corridor that, narrowing, continues through the valley of the Mackenzie River to the Arctic Ocean. They sweep through the southern half of Manitoba west of Lake Winnipeg, through half of Saskatchewan, and most of Alberta.

All of this lowland, in prehistoric times, was covered again and again by shallow seas. Each time the sea covered the land and receded again, it left a layer of fertile soil. So here is a level land of rich earth—a land of wheat fields and rich farms in its southern half and great forests toward the north.

The Cordilleran Mountain System

Some sixty million years ago came the period of mountain-building that lifted the mountains of the West. A broad band of them runs north and south parallel to the continent's Pacific Coast. In Canada they reach more than 400 miles inland from the Pacific. All together they make up the Cordilleran System, named from a Spanish word, *Cordillera,* that means "rope" or "chain." The Rockies are included in this system, along with the Mackenzies, toward the north, and all the other mountain chains that lie west of them.

Slowly, slowly, they were pushed up in range after interlocking range of towering, rocky peaks, with deep valleys lying between them. Some of the loftiest ranges in North America rose up near the coast, among them the ice-capped St. Elias Mountains that cross the southwest corner of Yukon Territory and the northwest corner of British Columbia. Here, in Yukon Territory, is Mount Logan, towering to 19,850 feet and second on the continent only to Alaska's Mt. McKinley.

The Cordilleran System is made up of the youngest mountains on the continent, and changes are still going on among them. Glaciers are still crunching down their slopes. In some places, the land is rising. Volcanoes to the south and along the Alaskan coast, and earthquakes all through the Cordilleran are evidence that the earth's surface here is still shifting.

The Pacific Coast

The load of Ice-Age ice pressed the Pacific Coast down, and then the melt-water flooded it, much as the Atlantic Coast was drowned. The western-most Coastal Mountains were flooded, with only their tops left above water. We see them today as hundreds of islands along the Pacific Coast of British Columbia and Alaska. Deep channels between the islands and slashing into the mainland are drowned valleys between the old mountain ranges.

The Frozen North

East of the Cordilleran, northern Canada is more or less level and is peppered with endless lakes, big and little. Dense forest dominates the land. Intermingling with forest, lake, and river are spreading areas of muskeg—swamps frozen solid through the winter but thawing in summer to give life to a rich variety of plants and animals.

The forests end at the "northern limit of trees"—a timberline that crosses the northern tip of Yukon, sweeps across the Mackenzie Valley almost at the Arctic Ocean, heads southeast to Hudson Bay, cuts across Quebec's Ungava Peninsula, and continues eastward to clip off the northern tip of Newfoundland. North of this timberline lies tundra, and barren rock and barren soil, and, finally, the Arctic Ocean with its immense raft of ice that floats around the North Pole.

During the long Arctic winter, the treeless tundra is frozen and almost lifeless, with temperatures of 50 degrees and more below zero. The frozen crust sweeps endlessly across the land, and across the water between the many islands—the storied home of Eskimo and polar bear. For a brief period, summer brings long, sunny days, when the ice melts, and there is open water between the islands and great stretches of water across the land.

Strangely, there is little rainfall—less, in some places, than in the Sahara—yet water is everywhere, in little ponds and big lakes, in swamps, in small streams and broad rivers. The water is there because, five or six or a dozen inches below the surface, the earth is still frozen. This is the "permafrost," where the earth is frozen solid and

never melts. Permafrost reaches downward in some places for hundreds of feet. Water cannot drain through it, and so the melt-water of summer stands on the surface. Plants cannot send roots into it, and so all the plants of the tundra are shallow-rooted and low-growing.

Summer brings a riot of sphagnum, and brilliant lichens. Tiny flowering plants shoot up, produce blooms and seeds, and wither and are gone again as the brief summer rockets by. Summer brings a great variety of animal life, too. Immense herds of caribou feed on the famous "reindeer moss" growing in mats over the land. There are ducks and geese and sea birds of many kinds. Muskrats and fish thrive in the thawed lakes and rivers. Insects feed on the animals or buzz around the brief flowers.

The Northeast Coast

Canada's northeast coast is formed by Baffin Island and the islands to the north, and by Newfoundland to the south. The Canadian Shield covers these and also reaches across Baffin Bay and Davis Strait to cover the big island of Greenland, underlying its several thousand feet of ice cap.

Along all these shores the land has been pushed up into rugged highlands, with high, forbidding cliffs against the sea. Rocky peaks rise several thousand feet above sea level. In the islands many peaks are more than a mile high and are ice-capped around the year. One theory of the formation of this land suggests that between the islands and Greenland an immense chunk of the Canadian Shield broke off and sank, allowing water to rush in and form Baffin Bay and Davis Strait, and letting the edges of the land spring upward into highlands. If this is true, the chunk sank a tremendous distance, for today these bodies of water are more than a mile deep in many places.

The coasts of the islands and of Newfoundland are deeply drowned, with thousands of islands just offshore, and the coastline is penetrated by innumerable inlets, bays, and sounds. Deep canyons carry swiftly-falling rivers from the land into the sea. Around the islands the waters are blocked through the winter until June by the Arctic ice pack. All through the year, Davis Strait and the Labrador Sea are likely to contain icebergs that have broken off—"calved"—from Greenland's ice-cap coast and drifted south, to melt at last in the warmer waters off the Island of Newfoundland.

River Systems

Wherever there is coastline in Canada—and there is an almost end-less amount of it—there are rivers that rush swiftly from icy inland lakes to the sea. In this flow of water to the sea, there are three great drainage systems.

The mighty St. Lawrence brings water down from the Great Lakes into the Atlantic Ocean. Along the way, many great rivers pour into it from the Shield, including the Ottawa and the Saguenay. West of the Great Lakes, the Saskatchewan-Nelson system brings water from the plains to Lake Winnipeg, then north into Hudson Bay. North of these flows the Mackenzie system, second in length on the continent only to the Mississippi. It includes the famous Peace, Athabasca, and Slave rivers and the Athabasca, Great Slave, and Great Bear lakes, as well as the Mackenzie River proper—a wide, wide river in a broad val-ley all the way from Great Slave Lake to the Arctic Ocean.

24

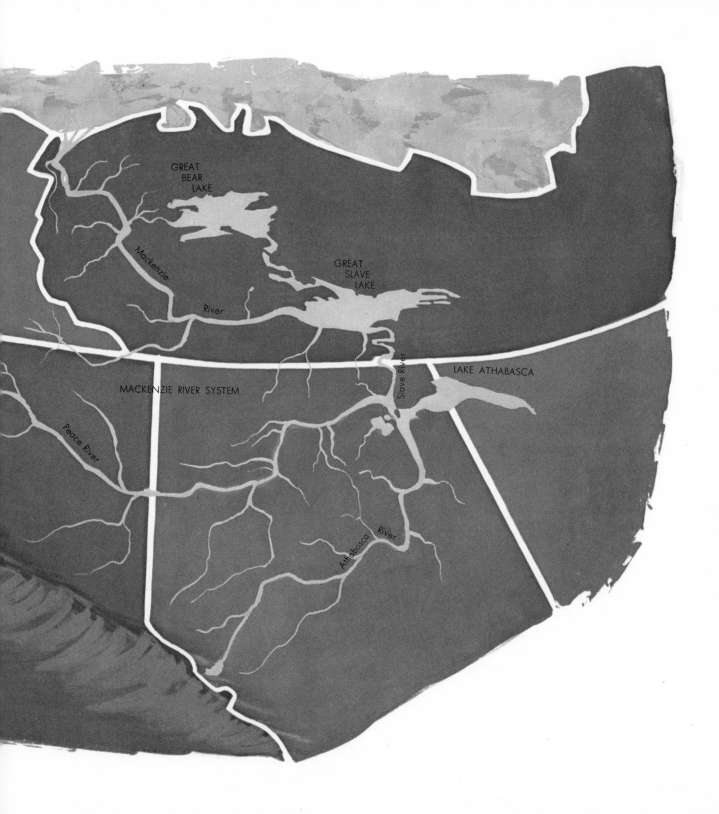

Climate of Canada

The wide variety of climate in Canada has led to the saying that almost anything can happen with weather and climate there, and almost always does. With a prevailing west-to-east wind direction, cold air flows from the Arctic southeastward to bring severe winters and chilly summers to most of the country. Yet hot winds move northeastward in summer to bring hot days to prairies, Shield country, and Atlantic provinces alike.

Balmy ocean currents bring warmth to the west coast, and moist Pacific winds blowing eastward strike the high mountains and drop their moisture. These same mountains protect the coast from the cold winds of the north. So the coastal region of British Columbia has a warm, very humid climate with mild winters.

Across the mountains to the east, however, the Prairie Provinces are much dryer and hot in summer, although the nights are usually cool. Here the winter winds scream down unhindered from the north, bringing blizzards and sub-zero temperatures. A few days after such a storm, a warm wind or "chinook" may sweep in from the south and quickly melt the snow and ice.

The Shield country of Ontario and Quebec is part of this great open interior through which winds can sweep, and so quick, sharp changes of weather are common here, too. Winters are severe, with snowfall of from 60 to 100 inches and more; summers are brief but pleasant. The climate is much milder in the Ontario and Quebec lowlands along the Great Lakes and the St. Lawrence River. Summers are longer and hotter, and winter cold is not so intense. Rainfall is greater, with an annual precipitation of more than 40 inches along the St. Lawrence.

The Maritime Provinces and Newfoundland are directly in the path of winds from the continent, and so they, too, have this "continental" climate—one that is produced by a large body of land and is not much affected by near-by water. There is heavy rainfall and winds are high. In spring and summer the influence of the sea is felt. Thick fog folds a heavy curtain about land and sea alike. The fog is formed far offshore, where the cold Labrador Current meets the warm Gulf Stream. It is a great danger to ships and to the Banks fishermen.

Northward across the forests of Canada the winter cold endures through longer and longer periods, with temperatures commonly dropping lower than 50 degrees below zero, and snowfall reaching 200 inches and more. North of permafrost, because there is little evaporation into the chilly air, the year's precipitation may be less than five inches. A few inches of snow fall, to lie throughout the winter or to blow away, but never to melt until the coming of the brief summer.

Things to think about

What are the major physical regions of Canada? How are they different from each other?

What activity in earth's formation created the Canadian Shield? Why was there no effect of erosion on this Shield as the seas ebbed and flowed over the North American Continent?

What effect did the ice ages have on the varied lands of Canada?

Why does the St. Lawrence River have ocean tides hundreds of miles inland?

What theory is suggested about the formation of Baffin Bay and Davis Straits?

Describe the big river-and-lake systems in Canada.

What ocean current warms the western coast of Canada?

People come to Canada

Across the Bridge

Scoured and belabored by moving ice in the Ice Age, and still most of it frozen throughout much of the year, with half its surface plastered with hard rock, this northern portion of North America does not seem to be a place where early man could live. Yet the first European explorers on this continent found people on it, from coast to coast. They were sometimes widely scattered, to be sure, but they had reached all parts of the continent, even the Arctic Circle.

Not quite all of the northern part of the continent was buried under ice during the Ice Age. Much of what is now Alaska was free and, probably, formed a land bridge from Alaska to the continent of Asia. Some 25,000 years ago or more, people may have begun to come across that bridge from Asia to North America. Small, brown people with straight black hair and dark eyes, they carried spears for which they had made sharp stone tips, and probably they knew the use of fire.

They may have followed game across the bridge. They hunted the giant mammoths and bears, the bison and camels and horses, and many other mammals that roamed the land and followed the ice northward as it receded—animals that finally died out, leaving their bones to tell their story. The people came afoot, the use of the horse was unknown to them except as game.

Through many centuries these people continued to come. They spread through Alaska and moved southward through mountain valleys that were sometimes ice free—along the Mackenzie Valley and on south, to leave the ice behind and travel the entire length of the continent. South of the ice some of them moved east along its edge, reaching the Atlantic and turning north again into southeast Canada. Some of them, instead of coming south from Alaska, moved eastward along Arctic shores all the way to Newfoundland and Greenland. So, very slowly, as the ice receded, people penetrated the portion of the continent that is Canada, and lived in scattered tribes and villages in almost every part of it.

The Eskimos

The people pushing eastward along Arctic shores were the Eskimos, who lived (and still live) on the tundra and the ice. They were (and are) masters of the harpoon for hunting whale and walrus, from which they drew food, oil for their efficient lamps for lighting and heating, sinews, skins, and bone that they used in a hundred ways.

Their boats were the one-man kayak, resembling a canoe that has been completely sealed over with skins, and the open umiak, a larger boat that carried several men.

In winter they built (and still build) beautifully engineered, weather-tight houses, called igloos, from blocks of ice. In summer they moved onto the warming tundras (and still do) for the seasonal hunting of the caribou, which migrate northward from the forests in herds of thousands.

31

Northwest Coast Indians

Descendants of the migrants who drifted south and spread across the continent all came to be called "Indians." However, they developed in different ways and at different rates, even in neighboring areas, until finally they were vastly different peoples. A language spoken in one part of the country was not understood in another. Different customs grew up, and ways of life developed, depending upon the kind of country in which they settled.

Along the northwest coast, the people were held near the coast by high, rugged mountains that came close to the sea. Here the climate was mild and life was fairly easy. Giant trees, especially cedars, grew in abundance, offering easy materials for use in daily living. The Indians carved fabulous canoes from them, used their wood for houses and their bark for clothing and blankets and containers, and carved other containers and tools and symbolic objects from the wood. There was wonderful fishing for salmon off the coast, around the islands, and in the big rivers that came down from the mountains; and the salmon could be dried and preserved for later use. This whole northwest coast area as well as Alaska, was occupied by Indians who fished for salmon and whales and seals and had plenty of time left over for "socializing."

The major social event was the "potlatch," a wintertime gathering called by the chief of some clan to announce or protect his prestige. In its course there were days of feasting, masked and costumed ceremony and entertainment, and giving of gifts. Guests were likely to arrive in giant canoes, which had high, carved bows brilliantly painted with clan symbols, and which were paddled by slaves. One potlatch demanded another in return (from which comes the term "Indian giving"), so that the winter was likely to be pretty well filled with such festivity.

The wooden totem pole is a hallmark of these Indians, developing, probably, from carving the cornerposts of the Indians' lodges, until finally giant separate poles stood in rows throughout the village. The poles were carved and brightly painted with images representing the important events of a chief's life, and were used to publish his importance and prestige.

Woodlands Indians

Moving up from the south and spreading westward from the Atlantic Ocean through more than half of Canada, came the many tribes of Woodlands Indians. The Micmac, in the Maritime Provinces and south of the St. Lawrence, were the first Indians to meet early European explorers. North of them were the Cree, who spread westward south of Hudson Bay. Still farther south of the Bay were the Ojibway; "Chippewa," the white man called them.

All of these and many more besides, belonged to the great Algonquian language family, their languages having similar qualities even though the tribes could seldom understand each other. In the great peninsula between the Great Lakes and the St. Lawrence River were the Huron. The Hurons were Iroquoian in language group, even though they were mortal enemies of the Iroquois tribes that lived south of them in what is now New York.

In the fertile lowlands of the Maritimes and the St. Lawrence, the Woodlands Indians were farming people. They raised corn and squash and potatoes and harvested wild rice, and lived in more or less settled villages where houses were rounded pole frames covered with bark. Northward, in deep forest and long months of snow, the Indians were nomads who hunted, trapped, and fished. Here the cone-shaped tepee was used, its poles and skin covering easily taken down, transported, and set up again as the Indians moved from place to place.

North, south, east, or west, these Indians were masters of the birchbark canoe, which they paddled up and down streams and across lakes throughout the land, and carried overland from lake to lake.

Plains Indians

On Canada's prairies, as on those of the United States, lived great herds of buffalo, or American bison. Hunting the buffalo, and depending on their flesh and hide and bone for food, clothing, shelter, and tools, were the Plains Indians. Chief among them in Canada were the Assiniboines, relatives of the Sioux and in the Siouan language group and, west of them, the Blackfoot Indians, who were Algonquian.

Here were a people who lived to travel and traveled to live, following the buffalo herds in hunting season and holing up in warm, sunny canyons when the weather turned bad. A whole village of handsome cone-shaped tepees might be pulled down in the course of a day, rolled into compact burdens along with all possessions, and be carted off to a new location.

For many centuries the Plains Indians, like the people of the north, used dogs to help move their burdens, packing them on the dogs' backs or using the travois. Centuries had gone by since horses had lived on this continent, and these people had never seen a horse.

Then, about 1540, both the explorers Coronado and De Soto rode into the southern fringes of the prairies of North America—rode horses into the prairies and left some of them. Before a hundred years had passed, horses had spread widely across the plains, and the Plains Indians rode them with the finest horsemanship the world has ever known. Here, certainly, was a boon to their way of life—quick and easy transportation and a fleet-footed ally for making war and hunting the ever-necessary buffalo. So it is that today a picture of the Plains Indian is not complete unless his horse is part of it.

Athapascan Indians

North of the Plains people, from Hudson Bay across Alaska and reaching into the tundra, is the land of the Athapascan Indians, including many such tribes as the Chipewyan, the Slave, and the Kutchin. These, too, were wanderers, moving their belongings on sleds that they pulled themselves. They hunted, not buffalo, but caribou, following great herds onto the tundra to take the season's meat, skins, and other supplies.

White Explorers from Across the Sea

A thousand years ago, the Norsemen, led by Eric the Red and his son Leif Ericsson, sailed from Scandinavia and established colonies in Iceland and Greenland. From there, they explored along the north Atlantic coast to North America, finding what they called "Helluland" or "land of great, flat stones," and, farther south, "Vinland," a verdant country lush with grapes. Centuries later, in 1492, Columbus

made his discovery of land far to the south—the West Indies.

Columbus and the others of his time were seeking something quite different from a new continent; the continent, in fact, was a barrier to their purpose. Across Asia from the countries of Europe lay China and India, with their rich spices and silks—materials that people could make fortunes with if they could bring them back to sell in Europe. But Asia was difficult to cross by land. How wonderful if a water route could be found across the top of the world!

So explorers' eyes turned northward across the Atlantic and into the Arctic Ocean, seeking a "Northwest Passage" into the Pacific. For 200 years this was the prime purpose of exploration around and across North America, while it slowly became evident that this new land was in itself a bigger prize than the Northwest Passage.

Encouraged by the success of Columbus, John Cabot reached the north Atlantic coast in 1497 and again in 1498. He sailed the New-foundland coast and landed on Cape Breton Island, claiming this Atlantic region for England. He reported fabulous fishing grounds, where fish could be caught simply by lowering baskets into the water; thereafter, summer after summer, the Grand Banks lured European fishermen across the water.

Exploring for France, Jacques Cartier in 1534 sailed through the Strait of Belle Isle, explored and named the Gulf of St. Lawrence, and landed on the Gaspé Peninsula to plant a flag and claim the region for France. The next year he sailed up the St. Lawrence River and came to a mountain-crested island. He visited a Huron Indian village, Hochelaga, on the island and named its mountain "Mount Royal," or, in French, *Mont Rèal*—which became the name of the city that eventually grew there. He could sail no farther up the river, because just above the island were swift rapids that stopped any ship. He named them "Lachine" (China) Rapids, and they are still called by that name. He called this new land "New France."

Other explorers continued the search for the water route across the top of the world; many of these were exploring for England. Sir Martin Frobisher in 1576 explored Frobisher Bay. Henry Hudson in 1610 discovered Hudson Strait and Hudson Bay. William Baffin in 1616 sailed Baffin Bay, and John Davis explored Davis Strait.

Father of Canada

While the search went on, there came to New France the man often called "Father of Canada"—Samuel de Champlain, adventurous and experienced French explorer and official geographer and map-maker for the French king. Champlain, too, was interested in a Northwest Passage; but he looked at the wonderful fishing grounds off north Atlantic shores and, inland, at the rich furs the Indians brought into their villages, and he knew that here was treasure as great as spices and silks.

In 1603 Champlain sailed the St. Lawrence River, and in 1604, he came again to New France to explore south of the gulf. He sailed into the Bay of Fundy, and established on its north shore a small colony that later moved across the bay to the present site of Annapolis Royal. This, called Port Royal, was Canada's first permanent settlement.

But Champlain's heart was with the St. Lawrence, and four years later he went back to the river to found a colony, high on a cliff overlooking the river; he called it *Québec*. This was a colony that grew and prospered through the years, to become the greatest of all French

strongholds in the new world. Champlain was its first governor, under a fur company organized by powerful French merchants; their purpose was to develop and control fur trade with the Indians throughout New France.

Champlain made friends with the Algonquian Indians all about him, and with the Hurons, farther west. He helped them fight off their old enemies, the Iroquois, earning the undying hatred of the Iroquois but cementing friendship with the Algonquians and Hurons. So they brought him furs and helped him explore. They taught him the use of their canoes and paddled with him up and down the rivers and through many lakes, carrying their canoes around rapids or from lake to lake; the Frenchmen called these carrying-places "portages." So Champlain learned the country; he discovered Lake Champlain, reaching far southward from the St. Lawrence; he explored the Ottawa River and Lake Nipissing, and went on to the shores of Georgian Bay and Lakes Huron and Ontario.

What he learned he put down in maps and written reports and took them, year after year, to France. So more colonists came, and more explorers. Champlain brought Jesuit priests to New France, who went into the Indian villages to establish missions; they taught the Indians and converted them to Christianity, at the same time learning about them and about the country. The priests wrote a careful record of what they learned, and it is today one of our best records of the settling of North America.

The Fur Trade Grows

Rapidly, a fabulous fur trade was building up. Into the St. Lawrence came many rivers from the north. West of the river, as we have seen, lay an immense system of great lakes, into which drained other northern lakes and rivers. Here were water highways through which trappers could travel, bringing in great canoe-loads of beaver and otter and fox pelts—furs that the northern cold had made thick and lustrous.

Indian trappers brought furs down to the Hurons by canoe; the Hurons moved them down the St. Lawrence to Montreal, where Champlain had built a big fur depot. Often the Hurons moved them all the way down to Quebec. Every spring, great fleets of Huron canoes filled the river at Montreal and Quebec. From the St. Lawrence, the furs went to Europe, where they brought high prices.

All of this was only begun in the lifetime of Champlain. He founded Trois Rivières in 1634 but died in 1635, too soon to see it become a great fur-trading center. A colony was founded at Montreal in 1642; the Jesuit priests and various explorers, headquartering there, reached farther and farther inland to establish missions and forts.

There was trouble, too, in New France. Lake Champlain extended southward deep into the land of the Iroquois. This long lake and the river from it into the St. Lawrence was the Iroquois' war trail, bringing them to the French colonies and to the Hurons. So the Iroquois often came raiding. In 1648 and 1649 they came in great waves against the Hurons, wiping out their villages, burning the missions, and killing Indians and Jesuits alike.

The St. Lawrence settlements survived, but they were in trouble, along with the fur company sponsoring them. The fur trade on which they depended was gone, without the Hurons; for a year or two, no Indian canoes came to the trading posts. Gradually, the fur trade grew up again. But the French king had had enough of fur companies, and in 1663 he took over New France as a royal colony.

Some of the Hurons had survived the onslaught of the Iroquois, and had pushed far west and north in their canoes, taking with them the knowledge of the white man's fur trade. Soon some of them were bold enough to bring furs again to the trading posts on the St. Lawrence.

The Jesuits were at work again, too, exploring and building missions; Marquette came from France, and Joliet, born in Quebec, teamed up with him to develop important missions like that at Sault Ste. Marie, and later to go far south down the Mississippi River and lay claim to the central part of the continent for France. Other explorers came from France. LaSalle came, and spent years exploring the Great Lakes and trading for furs, before he, too, turned to the Mississippi Valley.

In 1672 Count de Frontenac came to New France as its governor, and for 25 years he was a wise and courageous leader. He encouraged the explorers, and soon there were trading posts and missions all the way from Kingston (Ft. Frontenac) and Toronto to Fort William and Duluth. The fur trade prospered and grew immensely rich, and continued to grow all through the next century.

The Voyageurs

In 1731, La Verendrye and his "Voyageurs" came to map out a canoe trail far into the northwest. From Grand Portage on the west shore of Lake Superior (in what is now Minnesota) they portaged for nine miles around the falls of Pigeon River. When they finally put their canoes back in the river, they blazed a westward trail through the lakes to Rainy Lake and Rainy River and went on to discover Lake Winnipeg and push a canoe route farther and farther northward.

For many years the number of the Voyageurs grew, until there were hundreds of them; son followed father, until the Voyageurs became a legend. Year after year they pushed their canoes into the lonely reaches of the northwest and came back loaded with furs that the Indians had

traded to them. They carried the furs in great packs on their backs, and their canoes as well, across the portages and down that last long nine miles to Lake Superior. Here at the bustling village of Grand Portage was the eastern end of the "Voyageurs' Highway"; here the furs were transferred to larger canoes and moved across the Great Lakes to the St. Lawrence.

The colonies on the St. Lawrence became thriving trade centers, well settled and well fortified. Stores and schools, hospitals and hotels took care of the needs of their citizens. The ships of Europe brought them goods and waited in their harbors for outgoing cargoes of precious furs. Farms appeared in the lowlands near the river.

The English in New France

From the very beginning, English rivalry for power in the new world harassed the French. We have seen that before 1500 John Cabot sailed the Newfoundland coast and claimed the region for England. In the 16th and 17th centuries, rich fisheries developed along the coast in the Grand Banks, and they were dominated by England. But France had fisheries here, too.

First settlers in Acadia (now New Brunswick, Nova Scotia, and Prince Edward Island) were the French colonists on the Bay of Fundy; and Frenchmen continued to settle in Acadia, working the soil and developing fisheries. But as early as 1623 Scotch settlers also came to Acadia to colonize under English grants, thus naming Nova Scotia (New Scotland).

EARLY HALIFAX

South of Canada, along the Atlantic, Jamestown in Virginia and the Pilgrims and Puritans in Massachusetts already had established footholds of English colonization. From here in the years to come, the English took over the whole Atlantic Coast from Georgia to Maine.

To the north, British fur traders closely followed the explorers through Hudson Strait to the shores of Hudson Bay. Here, in 1670, was chartered the most famous fur company in the world, Hudson's Bay Company, which is still the big trading and fur company of Canada. Rivers drain into Hudson Bay from all directions, and down them came the Indian trappers, bringing in their furs. Here, direct to ocean-going ships, was a much quicker, easier route than the long arduous trip through the lakes and down the St. Lawrence.

The English competed with the French for furs from the northwest. Even along the St. Lawrence the English made allies of the Iroquois, and the Iroquois battled French and Huron to gain the fur routes.

In Europe, France and England were often at war, and their battles were often fought in the colonies. Even Quebec, the fortified heart of New France, was subject to British attack. In Acadia some places changed hands many times; Louisburg, French stronghold on Cape Breton Island, was one of these. Halifax in Nova Scotia was founded by the English and immediately became a thriving town—an English harbor and naval stronghold. Then France lost Acadia, and the British moved thousands of rebellious French colonists from this region, scattering them in colonies to the south. Longfellow's poem, *Evangeline,* tells the story of some of them who went all the way to Louisiana.

Finally, England and France waged their last great struggle for control of New France—a struggle that reached far south of Canada. This was the French and Indian War; from 1755 to 1763, many bloody battles were fought at various strategic points on the continent—at Fort Duquesne on the Ohio and at Crown Point; at Louisburg and at Fort Niagara. The Algonquian Indians sided with their friends, the French, and the Iroquois aided the English. The war ended with a great battle for Quebec, in which the generals for both sides were killed—Wolfe for the English and Montcalm for the French. England won the battle and took Quebec; and in 1763 the Treaty of Paris gave England all of New France that is now Canada.

English Canada

Although the country was now England's Canada instead of New France, the majority of the colonists were still French—60,000 strong. England did not force them to change; they held their lands as usual and were allowed their Roman Catholic religion. When the Revolutionary War started in 1775, in which the English colonies farther south fought for and won their independence from Great Britain, the Canadian colonies remained loyal to Britain. Thousands of loyal English moved across the border into Canada from the new United States. They founded such cities as Kingston (in what is now Ontario) and Saint John, in New Brunswick.

Gradually, Canada continued to develop. The fur trade boomed. Explorers charted more and more of the West and North. In 1778, Captain James Cook took his ships into the passages and harbors of Vancouver Island, on the Pacific Coast. The Hudson's Bay Company spread across the country and claimed ownership of thousands of square miles of western and northern wilderness, scattering their trading posts across it. Other fur companies rose in lively competition.

One of these was the North West Company, and one of its leaders was the Scottish trader and explorer, Alexander Mackenzie. Like many others, Mackenzie sought a route to the Pacific—the 300-year-old dream of a Northwest Passage. In 1789, he led a little fleet of canoes out of Great Slave Lake and downriver, northwest, but he came to the Arctic Ocean. By those who came after him, his name was given to river and mountains in this far northwest; but at the time he was bitterly disappointed that he had not reached the Pacific. He tried again in 1793, this time paddling up the Peace River from Lake Athabasca and crossing overland through the Rocky Mountains, with great toil and hardship. He came, finally, to the Pacific Coast, the first man to cross the continent. This time he wrote his name himself, triumphantly, and the date, July 22, 1793, on a great rock that lies offshore from Bella Coola.

After 1800, hundreds of thousands of new settlers came to Canada from the British Isles. The old harbor cities were thriving, and many others were growing up around the Great Lakes, along the St.

Lawrence, and on the Atlantic Coast. Down from the rich forests came millions of logs that lay in great rafts in the harbors, to be sawed into lumber and crushed into paper pulp. Here was an industry fully as rich as the fisheries and the fur trade. Canadian factories were supplying goods for Canadian people. Canadian shipyards were building boats and ships for use in Canadian waters, and the first canals were built to take them around the rapids on the rivers and between the lakes; the Lachine Canal was built above Montreal in 1825, and the first Welland Canal was started in 1827, to bypass

Niagara Falls between Lake Erie and Lake Ontario. The old water highway for the canoes of Indians and fur traders—even then the lifeline of Canada—already was beginning to change into the mighty St. Lawrence Seaway of today.

The *Royal William,* a steamer built at Quebec, sailed from Pictou, Nova Scotia in 1833, to become the first Canadian-built ship to cross the Atlantic. And in 1836 Canada's first railway began to operate, from Laprairie to St. John's in Quebec Province.

In those days the province was not called "Quebec." It was "Lower Canada," and Ontario was "Upper Canada." On July 1, 1867, these two combined in a confederation with Nova Scotia and New Brunswick, and took the names Quebec and Ontario; the Confederation was the beginning of a new nation—Canada. Queen Victoria had chosen Ottawa as its capital city.

The Confederation foresaw a nation that would reach from sea to sea, and gradually that came to pass. Canada bought the vast lands of the Hudson's Bay Company in the West and Northwest, and in 1870, Manitoba became the first province to be formed from them. British Columbia came next, in 1871, and Prince Edward Island in 1873.

Building much of the way through solid rock and vast reaches of wilderness, the Canadian Pacific Railway laid rails across the continent. The Railway brought thousands of settlers to the prairies and carried away the grain that they grew in this rich, black soil. By 1877, Manitoba was exporting wheat to Europe. The railway was completed across the continent in 1885. The prairies became a powerful element, and in 1905 Saskatchewan and Alberta became provinces in the Confederation. The Arctic north had already been ceded to Canada by England. In 1949 Newfoundland became a province, the last British territory in North America to become a part of Canada.

Canada was, in 1926, recognized by Great Britain as an independent nation. Her independence was won gradually and peacefully, but surely. She is a member of the British Commonwealth of Nations, whose members hold allegiance to the crown in a spirit of affection, respect, and mutual welfare, but who themselves carry on all the activities of any other free nation. They govern themselves, and pay their own way, and make their own destiny in peace or war with other nations.

Things to think about

What kind of people live in Canada today that lived there when explorers came from Europe?

Describe the typical houses they build, and tell why such "architecture" is used.

How was the way of life of the Indians of the Northwest Coast different from that of the Plains Indians? What gave them their livelihood? What was the mainstay of the Plains Indians? Of the Eskimos?

What part of Canada was at one time called "New France?"

During the long war between England and the French many French colonists were dispossessed by the English—can you name such a colony made famous in a poem?

Life in Canada today

Today's Canada is an immense nation occupying more than half a continent—yet her people live largely in a narrow "Main Street" along her southern border. Here, in hundreds of square miles, they have built their homes and farms, towns and cities, roads and railways. Northward lie thousands on thousands of square miles of wilderness where there are only widely scattered villages—mining towns and lumbering camps, fur-trading posts, and Indian and Eskimo villages.

Even in the cities, Canada's people live in close knowledge of the wilderness. Looking north from their office windows, they can see the green, forested highlands, the beginning of "the bush"—that land of deep forest, lakes and muskeg that spreads northward until it is stopped by permafrost. These are people of a frontier, looking north to bush and tundra for the conquests of tomorrow. This is a country that has just begun to grow. And to make it grow, they have around them all the machine-age wonders of today.

The St. Lawrence Seaway

Just as in the early years, the St. Lawrence River and the Great Lakes are Canada's lifeline. This vast system of water transportation reaches halfway across Canada. On it, to Canada's big cities, ships come from the harbors of the world, to be loaded with huge cargoes of grain and iron ore and paper and nickel and aluminum.

Canada and the United States have worked together to improve this waterway. Locks at Sault Ste. Marie take ships past the rapids between

Lake Superior and Lake Huron. The Welland Canal bypasses Niagara Falls, between Lakes Erie and Ontario. Most recent improvement is a magnificent system of new dams and locks on the river, between Kingston and Montreal, which greatly enlarge and deepen the channel. Big ocean ships once had to tie up at Montreal and transfer their cargo to smaller boats. Now they can travel all the way up the river and on through the Great Lakes to the big inland lake cities of Canada and the United States.

Today the St. Lawrence is, in truth, a "Seaway."

Manufacturing on the Seaway

Much of Canada's industry lies along the Seaway. The cities of Quebec and Montreal still rule the St. Lawrence, and their fine harbors, although hundreds of miles from the ocean, are alive with the world's ships. Today's Montreal is the largest city in Canada and one of the greatest seaports in the world. Those ships at her docks carry steel, copper, machinery, airplane parts, paper, textiles, chemicals, flour, sugar, tobacco, and many other products processed in her own mills and made in her own factories. Quebec is a world-famous center of newsprint manufacturing, of woodworking, of fur trade and tanning, of metal working; and from the days of the birch-bark canoe, she has been a builder of boats and ships.

In these cities and in others like Trois Rivières on the St. Lawrence —in Ottawa and Hull on the Ottawa River—in Toronto, Kingston, Hamilton, London, and Windsor on the Great Lakes—in almost every waterside city, in fact, including those that lie back on the many rivers —in all of these, manufacturing is either king or a powerful young princeling growing in importance with every year. The big south peninsula of Ontario between Lakes Ontario, Erie, and Huron holds so many manufacturing cities that it is Canada's greatest industrial center. Within it, the curving shore of Lake Ontario from Oshawa through Toronto and around to Niagara Falls is a "Golden Horseshoe" of industry.

Great quantities and varieties of goods are manufactured. Paper,

especially newsprint, leads them all. Canada produces far more newsprint than any other nation in the world. Almost any of her cities, from large to small, has its mills for reducing logs to paper pulp or for turning out the finished paper products. The world's largest newsprint manufacturing area is the vicinity of Shawinigan in the St. Maurice Valley, in Quebec. Lumber mills are important on the Seaway, too, as well as factories that turn out plywood and other wood products.

Immense amounts of metals are processed. Canada produces most of the world's nickel, and Sudbury, north of Georgian Bay, has long been the leading center for nickel smelting and refining. Canada is second only to the United States in the production of aluminum. Arvida, on the Saguenay River, early took the lead in aluminum manufacture. Canada's plants turn out a substantial amount of the world's lead, zinc, and copper; asbestos; uranium; gold, silver and platinum; and iron and steel.

Much of this metal is used on the spot in Canada, to manufacture automobiles and locomotives, refrigerators and farm machinery, watches and electrical equipment, and to make structural materials, like steel girders for bridges and buildings, and steel plates for ships. Go to almost any Seaway town or city, and you will find a metal-using industry at work, or a metal-processing industry, or both. Go to the "Lakehead," where Fort William and Port Arthur, on the west shore of Lake Superior, mark the head of the Seaway, and you will find shipbuilding and manufacturing of machinery (along with the inevitable paper-making). Go to Murdochville on the Gaspé Peninsula, at the mouth of the Seaway, and you will find smelters turning out a tenth of Canada's copper. All along the great ribbon of towns and cities in between, the metal plants thrive and grow in importance.

Other industries, too, lie along the Seaway. Sarnia, on Lake Huron at its passage into Lake Erie, heads "Chemical Valley," a giant complex of petroleum refineries, steel mills, and factories that turn out plastics, rubber, and chemicals. Many Seaway towns and cities are important in such food processing as meat-packing, canning of fruits and vegetables, and processing of dairy foods; in the manufacture of textiles and clothing; in the processing of furs and leather.

Main Street: 4,000 Miles

Great as it is, the Seaway is only part of the story of Canada's industry. This story runs 4,000 miles along "Main Street"—from one ocean to another. St. John's, far out on the tip of Newfoundland, is on a fine Atlantic harbor. Here they build ships and boats, mill lumber, process fish, and manufacture marine engines, fishing equipment, clothing and chemicals. Corner Brook on Newfoundland's west coast has important paper mills and iron foundries.

Nova Scotia's Halifax is important for meat packing, shipbuilding, oil refining, fish processing, and other industries. Up the coast in the Sydney-Glace Bay area, ships are built, metals are processed, and chemicals are manufactured. These are only a few of the manufacturing points in the Atlantic Provinces; Charlottetown in Prince Edward Island, Moncton and Fredericton and Saint John in New Brunswick, process foods or wood or metals and manufacture finished goods from them.

54

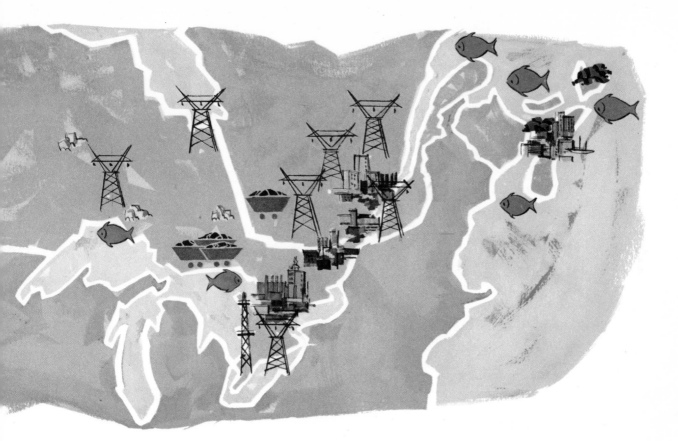

Look west along "Main Street" from Lake Superior, and find still more of the story. Winnipeg, in Manitoba, is Canada's gateway to the West—a great city of commerce and manufacturing, of meat packing and flour milling, of oil refining and paper making and lumbering, of metal working and railroad shops and the manufacture of railroad equipment. Regina and Saskatoon, the big cities of Saskatchewan, have meat-packing plants and cereal factories, oil refineries, chemical factories, wood-working and metal-working plants.

Calgary and Edmonton, in Alberta, are stand-out cities in the refining of petroleum. Both cities are centers of an immense system of refineries that continue to spring up like mushrooms. In British Columbia, Trail has the world's largest lead and zinc smelter; and Vancouver and Victoria have pulp and paper mills, lumber mills and woodworking, fish packing and canning, shipbuiding, and many other industries.

The Raw Materials

With one important exception—aluminum—these products of Canada's industry are made directly from her own raw materials. Her supply of raw materials is tremendous. Immense petroleum fields in Alberta spread out from Calgary and Edmonton and feed the great refineries; they supply most of the oil that Canada uses. In the cities of Medicine Hat, Lethbridge, and Pincher Creek in Alberta, and Fort St. John on the Peace River in British Columbia, are some of the world's largest natural-gas fields. Pipelines carry oil and gas to Sarnia and other points on "Main Street," to frontier towns, to United States cities. By-products of the oil fields include sulphur and fertilizers, and various chemicals used in plastics manufacture.

Farms and ranches produce some of the raw materials. Big cattle ranches on the prairies and in the rich, protected valley of British Columbia are the reason for the busy meat-packing plants in western cities. Across the Prairie Provinces sweep vast wheat fields—so look for flour milling, for huge elevators where grain is stored, for ships loaded to capacity with wheat, at Vancouver, at the Lakehead, at Montreal and Quebec. In the "Ontario Peninsula," in the St. Lawrence lowlands, in Nova Scotia and New Brunswick and especially in Prince Edward Island, are such prosperous vegetable farms, orchards, and dairy farms that much of their industry rests on processing these foods.

Fisheries, too, supply raw materials. Among the most important fishing grounds of the world, the Grand Banks off Newfoundland and other fisheries of the Atlantic Provinces supply immense quantities of cod, salmon, herring, and lobster for canning and processing plants. On the Pacific Coast, salmon and herring are the major catch; and on many inland lakes, whitefish and other lake fish are caught and canned or frozen.

Forests are a treasure-trove of raw materials—and forests cover more than half of Canada. Along British Columbia's humid coast grow the biggest fir and spruce trees in all the lumbering industry; and all the way across Canada, fir and spruce and pine, from "Main Street" to permafrost, supply logs for pulpwood and lumber. One of the commonest sights in Canada is a great raft of logs "stored" in a harbor, or being towed across a lake, or being floated down a river—thousands on thousands of logs held together by a "boom," a chain of logs that goes all the way around them. Look for these big rafts in the harbors of Vancouver, the Lakehead, Ottawa, Montreal, Quebec, Corner Brook —and on rivers like the Nipigon, floating down from the bush where the logs are cut, to the harbors where they're milled.

Canada exports pulpwood; so add logs to the cargo of the big ships that travel the Seaway. And add, too, sixteen million Christmas trees a year, cut in every province.

Furs are still important today. Many of the northern towns are headquarters and supply points for Indian and Eskimo trappers, who take fox, mink, muskrat, ermine, and others in great numbers; fox and mink are raised commercially in "fur farms" in every province. Seals are top catch in Arctic Ocean waters, where they are industriously hunted by the Eskimos.

Metals Are Raw Materials

Nickel, copper, uranium, iron, gold, zinc, lead, and silver—important in that order—are a major part of Canada's raw materials. Canada is a rich storehouse of metal-bearing ores. The rock of the Canadian Shield is part of the storehouse. The Rocky Mountains of the west are part of it. The frozen north is part of it. The great plains and the St. Lawrence lowlands and the Atlantic Provinces all share in it.

At Sudbury, in Ontario, there are large nickel smelters that break down the ore and take the metal from it and refine it. All around those smelters are the richest nickel mines the world has known, and important mines of silver, gold, and platinum, of lead, zinc, and copper as well. Canada's own mines supply raw materials for her industry.

Newfoundland has iron, lead, copper, silver, and zinc mines; iron mines on Bell Island reach under the sea. The ore from them is loaded on ships at Wabana and sent to Sydney, in Nova Scotia, because coal is required for the super-hot blast furnaces that melt iron from ore, and there are coal mines near Sydney. So Sydney, instead of Wabana, is a steel city.

Quebec's Gaspé Peninsula has rich copper mines that supply the big smelter area at Murdochville. South of the St. Lawrence, in the Sherbrooke-Thetford Mines area, much of the world's asbestos is mined; and here, too, is copper.

Almost all of Quebec and Ontario provinces lie in Canadian Shield country, where the storehouse is often fabulously rich. At Knob Lake, near the Quebec-Labrador border, Schefferville is the center of immense deposits of iron ore. The ore is sent by railroad to Sept Iles on the St. Lawrence River, where it is loaded on ships for transport to the blast furnaces of Canada and other countries. At Rouyn in western Quebec, and across the line in Ontario at Kirkland Lake and Timmins, gold and copper and zinc are mined. In the Kirkland Lake area, straight north of the great Sudbury nickel mines, are some of the richest gold mines in the world. West of Sudbury at Elliot Lake, there are important mines of pitchblende, a uranium ore. Iron mines north of Sault Ste. Marie and Fort William send their ore to Great Lakes steel centers.

All the way west, in British Columbia, the Kimberley and Trail areas have rich silver, lead, and zinc mines that feed their smelters.

These are some of Canada's largest mines; there are many others. Many of them are in or near "Main Street," in a part of the storehouse that is more or less easily entered and worked. By truck and railway and ship, they dump their ore at the doors of smelters and blast furnaces in the midst of Canada's industry.

What about the rest of the storehouse—those thousands of square miles of the north? To look north is to find gold, copper, silver, lead, and zinc all the way to British Columbia's western border and widely scattered over Yukon Territory; here Dawson centers the famous gold fields of the Klondike. Straight east in Northwest Territories is Port Radium, on Great Bear Lake, centering important uranium mines. To the southeast, Yellowknife on Great Slave Lake is a famous gold-mining town—the largest town, with 3,500 people, in the Northwest Territories. On the south shore of Great Slave Lake, around Pine Point, lies an immense unworked field of high-grade lead and zinc.

Look north in Saskatchewan, at Lake Athabasca, and find one of the world's greatest uranium fields, around Eldorado and Uranium City. In northern Manitoba are two new enormously rich nickel discoveries, at Lynn Lake and Thompson. And south of those important iron mines at Schefferville is a new discovery of even greater iron fields, this time just over the line in Labrador, at Labrador City on Wabush Lake.

These are some of the important mines of Canada's deep wilderness. For the most part they are new discoveries; the towns are new towns, still developing—towns with modern homes and stores and good schools. They are communities of people who take the ore from the mines and ship it to civilization, or, often, smelt it and ship the concentrates. On a vast frontier, they are Canada's pioneers of today; they are "opening up the north."

Transportation

First requirement for "opening up" new country is a means of transportation—a means for taking people into it and bringing out its products. The St. Lawrence Seaway has filled this need, both in exploring and developing the country and in carrying on the rapidly-growing commerce of today. The Prairie Provinces were added to Canada after the Canadian Pacific Railway was finished from the Atlantic to the Pacific Coast in 1885.

Today there are two great railway systems that operate all the way across Canada, from one coast to the other. They serve the cities and towns of "Main Street" and run north through the prairies to Saskatoon and Edmonton. One line runs across southern Quebec and central Ontario, blasted for hundreds of miles through the hard rock of the Canadian Shield, to serve the towns of this rich mining country.

Branch railways lead to many important points in the north. One, for example, serves the iron fields at Schefferville and Wabush Lake. A railway goes all the way from Regina, in Saskatchewan, to Churchill, on Hudson Bay, where the wheat it brings from the prairies is loaded on ships for Europe, and so the distance the wheat has to travel is reduced by 1,000 miles. The same railway early served The Pas and Flin Flon, centers of mining and smelting, lumbering and fur trapping, in northern Manitoba; branches lead from it to those important new nickel fields at Lynn Lake and Thompson.

A railway goes from Edmonton to Waterways, in northern Alberta, and from there steamboats travel the Athabasca River and Lake Athabasca, to supply Uranium City and the other towns on the lake. A new 438-mile railway to be built north from Grimshaw, Alberta, will bring better transportation to Great Slave Lake and help to open the lead and zinc mines that are waiting there.

Railways are slow to build, and boats on river and lake are summer things, gone with the winter freeze. In this northern wilderness of forest and treacherous muskeg, of hard rock and ice and snow, of great distances, airplanes are an invaluable means of transportation. Canada's daring "bush pilots" have been famous since early development of the airplane, often risking their lives to fly into settlements

that were stranded and in need of help. As airplanes improved, they became more and more important in the north. Now, all the way south from the Arctic Ocean, the frontier towns have good airports, and the airplane is often their only contact with civilization. Their food and supplies, tools and machines are flown in; their sick are flown out to hospitals; their uranium and gold and furs are flown to "Main Street." Scheduled flights reach some of the northernmost settlements, including Inuvik, near the Arctic Ocean in the northwest corner of Northwest Territories. This is a town recently built by the government to serve a tremendous area of fur trapping and minerals exploration.

Air routes, of course, cross all of settled Canada. Every big city has its modern airport. Montreal's, for example, is a leading international airport, and planes come into it from many American and European cities.

Good roads have long been the pride of settled Canada, and one of the best is the recently-completed Trans-Canada Highway, which travels the center of "Main Street" from coast to coast. The Alaska Highway connects with the main north-south highway through British Columbia at Dawson Creek and runs northwest through British Columbia and Yukon Territory to Fairbanks, Alaska. A thrilling feat of rugged engineering, this is the first continental highway into Alaska.

Power

Still another factor in the development of Canada—and especially of her great manufacturing plants—is that she has almost unlimited possibilities for electric power. Hundreds of rivers come roaring down from the Canadian Shield; power dams and hydroelectric plants built on such rivers convert the force of their falling water into electricity.

The Seaway dams on the St. Lawrence are power dams, and many important power plants lie along the river. Up the Ottawa River, its power is harnessed at Ottawa and Hull. At Trois Rivières and Shawinigan Falls on the St. Maurice River, and at Chicoutimi and Arvida on the Saguenay, cheap power from these two rivers turn the wheels of a great variety of manufacturing plants.

A substantial amount of the world's aluminum is turned out in Canada, but not a pound of aluminum ore—bauxite—comes from Canada.

The power resources on these two rivers are so great and so cheap that bauxite can be shipped in for this immense aluminum-processing industry.

In Newfoundland the development of water-power has only just begun. Grand Falls, deep in wilderness on the Hamilton River, is being harnessed. The falls and several sets of rapids make up a drop in this big river of more than 1,000 feet. Newly-built power plants at the falls and on some of the tributaries will send electricity south to eastern Canadian cities, and will hasten the development of those iron mines and foundries at Wabush Lake, only a little way west of Grand Falls.

West of the St. Lawrence, the most famous source of power is Niagara Falls, where the waters of the Great Lakes take a 160-foot tumble as they travel the Niagara River between Lakes Erie and Ontario. There is much available water power in Canada, on the swift rivers that empty into the Seaway; on northern rivers that flow to Hudson Bay; on the Winnipeg and Nelson and Saskatchewan rivers of the Prairie Provinces; on the rivers of the Territories—the Yukon and the Mackenzie and those that flow into Great Slave Lake.

British Columbia may have the richest potential of all, in her streams that flow swiftly from the mountains; famous among these are the Peace and Columbia rivers. Famous, too, is Kitimat, aluminum-manufacturing center on a deep channel to the Pacific, where bauxite can be brought in and aluminum taken out by ship. But Kitimat needed power. Back in the mountains, a chain of lakes flowed east for a hundred miles. So the Kenney Dam was built across the eastern end of the chain, and a 10-mile tunnel was built at the western end, into the Kemano River, to let the water flow west instead of east and fall into the river. Here, under ground, the power plant was built that supplies electricity for making aluminum at Kitimat.

Coal, too, supplies energy for making electricity, in many plants throughout Canada. Coal comes from southern British Columbia and Alberta, and from Nova Scotia. And at Ontario's Douglas Point, on Lake Huron north of Sarnia, near Kincardine, Canada's first atomic-energy plant for producing electrical power is being developed.

63

The People

Nowhere in the world is the influence of a country's origin more plainly written than in Canada. When the French surrendered Canada to Great Britain, there were 60,000 French in New France—mostly in the colonies along the St. Lawrence. Today their descendents are more than five million strong—nearly one-third of the total population of

Canada. They speak French, and very little English; they have kept their French customs and traditions, and their religion—the Roman Catholic. Quebec is their special province, but they live in all the others; St. Boniface, near Winnipeg, for example, is a French town.

Living alongside this French culture and mingling with it are people of English background who make up about one-half of Canada's population. Many are descendents of early English settlers, especially those who moved from the United States at the time of the Revolutionary War. Others arrived in more recent years, pouring into Canada in such numbers as to add several million to her population.

So Canada has two main cultures and two languages, French and English, and that is of great importance to her people. In the federal courts and in the Parliament, both languages are used; when Queen Elizabeth II visits Canada and speaks to Parliament, she speaks in English, then repeats what she has said in French. Stamps and government documents are printed in both languages. Recipes and directions appear in both English and French on packaged foods and other goods. On the street a sign may read both "ECOLE" and "SCHOOL."

Other nationalities, too, are important in Canada. The Scotch came early to Nova Scotia, and that province is still strongly Scottish. The Irish came to New Brunswick and Ontario; German, Ukrainians, Scandinavians, Dutch, and Poles are important members of the population.

Canada has 185,000 Indians, most of them living in reserves (reservations) all across Canada; and about 12,000 Eskimos. Except in three or four towns (Inuvik is one), they do not intermingle; the tree line is, in general, the northern limit for the Indians and the southern limit for the Eskimos. Some of them live in the old way, much as they have always lived; others are learning modern ways, based, often, on the use of modern machines. In many of their communities, co-operatives are centers for learning as well as for marketing their goods.

Indians operate well-managed commercial fisheries on the shores of many northern lakes, as well as the famous fisheries of the Pacific Coast. Eskimos now lash their one-man kayaks to the deck of a big power boat, a dozen of them at a time, and do their fishing and seal-hunting from this efficient base. And Eskimos made up the first oil-drilling crew to work in Arctic Canada.

The Arts in Canada

The theater is foremost in the arts in Canada, and foremost in the theater is the Stratford Festival. In this summer season at Stratford, Ontario, Shakespearean and other plays are so well produced that the festival is world-famous. Other leading professional groups include the Crest Theatre of Toronto and the Manitoba Theatre Centre, in Winnipeg. There are several fine French companies in Montreal; one of these is the well-known Théatre du Nouveau Monde, which every year makes an extensive tour in Canada and abroad. There are active amateur groups working in all the provinces and entering an annual competition, the Dominion Drama Festival.

Festivals are a lively part of all the arts in Canada. That at Stratford is expanding to include music, painting exhibits, books, and handicrafts; arts exhibits from French Canada were a recent feature. Two other major summer festivals, one at Montreal and one at Vancouver, offer orchestra and solo concerts by world-famous artists, and ballet, opera, and theater.

Music in a Canadian city often centers around a symphony orchestra, whether it is the world-famous orchestra of Montreal or Toronto, or that of a much smaller city or town where the musicians work at it in their spare time. An interesting development in recent years is the National Youth Orchestra, made up of more than 100 young players who come from all parts of Canada to play in Toronto, or at the Stratford Festival, or at points along an organized tour. Also important to young musicians is Les Jeunesses Musicales du Canada, an organization that helps them find places in orchestras, sponsors a summer music camp near Montreal, and conducts an annual National Music Competition with fine musical opportunities open to the winners.

Opera and ballet both have fine companies that perform each season in the larger cities. Chief among them is the Canadian Opera Company, which has an annual season in Toronto and also tours some of the smaller cities.

Canadian painting and sculpture are exhibited throughout Canada, at local festivals and shows as well as at such art centers as the National Gallery of Canada in Ottawa and the Montreal Museum of Fine Arts, where world masterpieces are exhibited.

Literature in Canada includes many volumes of poetry, fiction, history, and biography. Canada's rugged land and thrilling history furnish material for many of these. Headliners in the nineteenth century were two French-Canadians, Alfred Garneau, who wrote the history of New France, and Philippe de Gaspé, historical novelist; and the English John Richardson, who wrote about the Pontiac conspiracy in *Wacousta*, and Thomas Chandler Haliburton, sometimes called "Father of American humor"; his most famous work is *The Clockmaker, or The Sayings and Doings of Sam Slick*. Charles W. Gordon (his real name was Ralph Connor) won fame at the end of the century with his novels of expanding Canada, *Sky Pilot* and *The Man from Glengarry*. Earlier than these are thrilling accounts of Canada's exploration by such men as Cartier, Champlain, Mackenzie, and the Jesuit priests.

In more modern times, writers who are internationally famous include Canada's great humorist, Stephen Leacock; Mazo de la Roche, who wrote the *Jalna* series; Frederick George Scott and many other poets writing about Canada; Ernest Thompson Seton, who wrote *Krag, the Kootenay Ram* and other fine animal stories; and L. M. Montgomery, who wrote the *Anne of Green Gables* series. There are many others.

There is a great variety in the handicrafts, from the skillful weaving and pottery-making of the Atlantic Provinces to the wood-carving, beading, and basketry of the Indians. Go to the Nova Scotia Festival of Arts and Crafts at Tatamagouche, to see complex and beautiful weaving; go to the Pacific Coast, to find Indians still carving totem poles and weaving Chilkat blankets. From the north come exquisite carvings in ivory and soapstone done by the Eskimos, who always, since their history is known, have excelled in intricate carving. Today

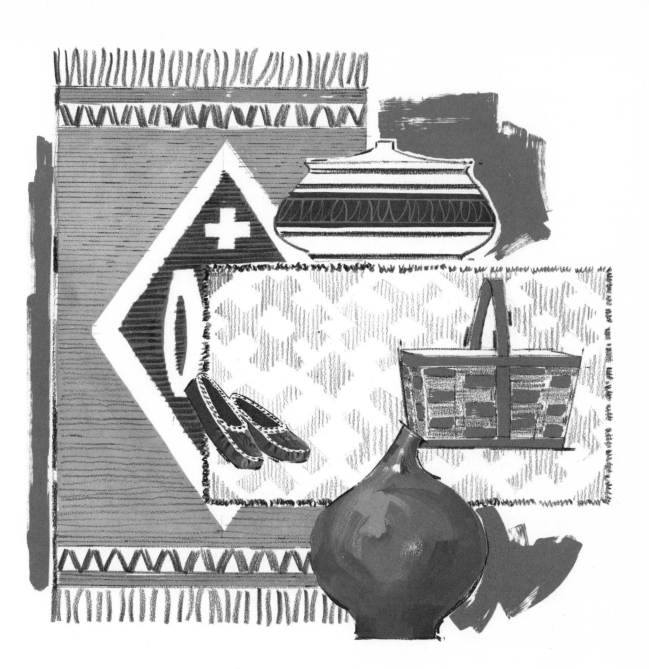

they are learning to make fine decorative prints; their co-operative at Cape Dorset on Baffin Island, near the Arctic Circle, is a center for this art, and prints have gone from there around the world.

Canada's Government

Canada has a Federal Government that is a democratic parliamentary system; its laws are made by a parliament controlled by the people. Its capital, where Parliament meets, is at Ottawa.

Queen Elizabeth II, as head of the Commonwealth of Nations, is Queen of Canada and head of the Canadian State. She is represented in Canada by the Governor General, who is appointed on the advice of Canada's Prime Minister.

Parliament is made up of the Queen, the Senate, and the House of Commons. The Senate has 102 members appointed for life, on the recommendation of the Prime Minister. There are 265 members of the House of Commons, and they are elected by the people of Canada, for a term of not more than five years.

The people vote in several political parties, the Progressive Conservative, the Liberal, the New Democratic and the Social Credit. After an election, the political party with the majority of members in the House of Commons is in control of the government, and its leader becomes Prime Minister. If at any time he comes into disagreement with a majority of the House, his government falls, and a new election is held, choosing a new House and a new Prime Minister.

The Federal Government controls such matters of over-all importance as trade and commerce, finance, defense, and world-relations. But each province has its own provincial government (and its own capital), to regulate matters more closely allied to the community, such as education and the holding of property. The territories are governed by commissioners appointed by the Federal Government, with the help of councils elected by the territories.

Canada's "Mounties"

The Royal Canadian Mounted Police are known affectionately throughout Canada as "The Mounties"; they are one of the proudest traditions of Canada. They were organized in 1873 as a police force on horseback. Soon, in posts that they established across the land, these almost indestructible men in red jackets became a symbol of good police work and friendly service to the law-abiding citizens. They were especially heroic throughout the territories, where for many years they were almost the only contact that some settlements had with civilization.

Today, 4,500 strong, they work throughout Canada. Their means of getting about is largely motorized—motorcycle, car, or airplane; but a horse-mounted troop is often a gay red splash in a parade or official celebration.

Education and Research

Canada's young people go to excellent schools—and they all go; ninety-seven percent of her people can read and write, the world's finest record. Each province is responsible for its own schools, and in each one, education is a matter of importance and prideful accomplishment. Schools may be new, modern buildings in cities, easily reached; or one-room country schools, reached by bus; or, as in northern Ontario, a school on wheels—a railway car that moves from one community to another. An interesting feature is an exchange program by which students from French Canada and from English Canada visit back and forth, to learn the ways of each other's schools, homes and cultures.

Success on another front is the increasing degree of education of Indians and Eskimos, in which they not only learn the fundamentals but learn trades and business management as well. The big, modern school built by the Federal Government at Inuvik is a fine example of the development in education in the North.

Among Canada's fine universities and colleges are its oldest, Laval University in the city of Quebec, founded in 1635, and its largest, the University of Toronto. Other leaders are McGill University at

Montreal, famous especially for its school of medicine; the French-Canadian *Université de Montréal;* Queen's University at Kingston, Ontario, famous for its school of mines; the law school of Dalhousie University, in Nova Scotia; and the University of Western Ontario, in London, Ontario, with its fine medical and business administration courses.

Through the years, dramatic successes in research have come from Canadian centers. The first telephone was used by Alexander Graham Bell in Brantford, Ontario, in 1876. The first trans-Atlantic wireless message was received from England by Marconi at St. John's, Newfoundland, in 1901. Sir William Osler, Canadian physician and teacher, was a graduate of McGill, and there and in other Canadian centers he made discoveries and developed practices that greatly influenced the whole profession of medicine. Sir Frederick Banting, while at the University of Toronto, was one of the discoverers of insulin.

Through the National Research Council, hundreds of scientists are at work on research in biology, chemistry, physics, engineering, and medicine. Research on the use of atomic energy has an important center at Chalk River, on the Ottawa River north of Ottawa.

The DEW Line

The DEW line is another kind of policing, carried on by the United States and Canada. It is a series of radar stations forming a line across the Arctic from Alaska, south of Point Barrow, to Baffin Bay; the line is roughly parallel to the Arctic Circle and about 100 miles north of it.

DEW is the initials of Distant Early Warning. Its stations are manned by soldiers and aircraft pilots who are the northernmost line of defense against any attack that might be made on the North American continent.

Things to think about

Describe what can be called "Main Street" in Canada.

What three major areas in Canada are still largely wilderness? What conditions in them have discouraged settlement? How are machines helping to conquer those conditions?

What natural resources, working together, have developed Canada's industry and made her a strong nation?

Is the development of Canada's resources complete, or is it just beginning? Where do Canadians look today for new resources?

What were Canada's earliest travelways?

How many languages are used consistently in Canada?

Who are some of Canada's famous authors?

How is the government of Canada related to Great Britain?

Can you trace the DEW line on a map?

Enchantment of Canada

Canada has so many different kinds of enchantment, spread over such tremendous distances, that it takes years of visiting to become familiar with them all. Canada is a land of three oceans and much big water in between. Canada is a land of mountains and plains, of lake-side and river valley, of rock and far-flung forest wilderness and tundra; of ice and snow, and yet of hot summer sun and an almost tropical Pacific Coast. Canada is a land of big cities and big ships and big factories, of towns and mining camps and farms and huge wheat and cattle ranches. Canada, for certain, is a land of many kinds of enchantment.

Playgrounds for the Public

Anyone who has ever heard of national parks in the Rockies has heard of Banff National Park and its neighbor to the north, Jasper National Park, in the rugged heart of Alberta's Rocky Mountains. These two have probably the world's finest assortment of towering peaks, live glaciers, sparkling lakes, rivers, and waterfalls, and good roads and foot trails to make their enchantment accessible. Beautiful Lake Louise in Banff is that park's hallmark; and besides the wonderful mountain scenery, Banff is famous for its swimming pools with mineral water that comes out of the ground piping hot. Here, too, is the annual Indian Days celebration. Indians in heavily-beaded native dress set up gay tepees and conduct four days of tribal dances and horse racing and other contests.

JASPER NATIONAL PARK

The spectacle of Jasper National Park is climaxed by such features as Athabasca Falls, in the Athabasca River, near the highway; and Mount Edith Cavell, where Angel Glacier spreads its wings. Both parks are centers for superb winter sports, with championship ski meets and colorful winter carnivals.

The highway from Banff to Jasper goes through the Columbia ice fields, skirting the famous Athabasca Glacier; this is one point of several in Canada where a ride on an "icemobile" across a glacier gives the traveller a closeup view of it.

Banff is bordered on the west by two national parks in British Columbia, Yoho and Kootenay; two more, Glacier, and Revelstoke, lie a little farther to the west. Each of them a wonderland of mountains, rivers, canyons, and forests, they are becoming popular as good roads come to them. The new Trans-Canada Highway travels through all except Kootenay, and through Banff as well; Kootenay has a paved highway that connects with it.

South of these, as the Alberta-United States line, is Waterton Lakes National Park, an area famous for sparkling lakes and interesting wild-life. It is part of the Waterton-Glacier International Peace Park, which continues through Glacier National Park in the United States, just across the line.

The Atlantic Provinces have several fine national parks. Cape Breton Highlands, at the northern end of Cape Breton Island, is a landscape of green valleys, forested, rolling hills, and rocky headlands meeting the shores of the Atlantic and the Gulf of St. Lawrence—a fine setting for beach fun, fishing, boating, hiking, and scenic drives. Fundy National Park, on the southeast shore of New Brunswick, is a forested, 1,000-foot-high tableland with lovely lakes and rivers. Its shoreline is the Bay of Fundy, where tremendous tides pound sheer sandstone cliffs. Prince Edward Island National Park preserves miles of gulf beaches along the Island's north shore. The island is the setting for the *Anne of Green Gables* books; "Green Gables," Anne's home, is a tearoom in the park. Terra Nova National Park is an oceanside park on the east side of the Island of Newfoundland, skirted by the east end of the Trans-Canada Highway.

The St. Lawrence Islands National Park is made up of 14 of the many beautiful islands in the St. Lawrence River near Kingston; these islands are for public use, for picnicking, boating, fishing and beach fun. So are the 42 islands of Georgian Bay Islands National Park, off the southeast shore of Ontario's Georgian Bay; hiking trails here are especially rich in wildlife. Point Pelee National Park, jutting into Lake Erie south of Windsor, is another area dedicated to public beaches and water recreation.

Riding Mountain National Park in Manitoba and Prince Albert National Park in Saskatchewan are northern areas of deep forest and beautiful lakes; reached by good roads, they are popular with campers and other vacationers.

Many national historical parks preserve the history of Canada, especially in remains or replicas of old forts. Some of these parks in Nova Scotia are the Louisburg Fortress; the Halifax Citadel; a replica near Digby of Champlain's original settlement, Port Royal; Grand Pre, north of Wolfville, where lived the Acadians of *Evangeline;* and the Alexander Graham Bell Museum at Baddeck. In every province highlights of its history are preserved in parks such as these.

Two national parks were established especially as game refuges. The 17,000-square-mile Wood Buffalo Park, shared by Alberta and the Northwest Territories, is an area of great variety; it includes both forest and plains, has big Lake Claire and the Peace River, and on its boundary, Lake Athabasca and the Athabasca and Slave rivers. Here is a fabulous wealth of wildlife—buffalo and bear, caribou, deer, and moose, and smaller animals and water fowl of many different kinds. This is the home of the few remaining woodland bison, survivors of the Ice Age; they are larger than the prairie buffalo and without the hump.

Elk Island National Park is also in Alberta, but nearer civilization, just east of Edmonton; it is a preserve for elk, moose, deer, and buffalo.

Every province has many provincial parks, which vary greatly in size and development. Many are small roadside parks primarily for the camper and picnicker, perhaps on a stream or lake with beach and fishing. Others are giant-size. One of these is Ontario's Algonquin, where in nearly 3,000 square miles of lakes and forest, there are fishing and canoeing and hiking. Another, still wilder, is in western Ontario—the Quetico, which, adjoining America's Superior National

Forest, helps to make up the far-famed Superior-Quetico Canoe Country, a roadless wilderness penetrated only by canoe. A new 4,000-
square-mile provincial park is being developed in the Killarney region,
north of Georgian Bay.

Wildlife

Canada's forests hold enough different kinds of wildlife to fill many books about them. Probably none of these is better known than the moose, that huge-antlered, awkward-looking member of the deer family; he is found almost anywhere in Canada where there are lakes and forest. Also common to most of the forests are black bear, deer, lynx, bobcat, wolf, mink, otter, muskrat, fox, beaver, porcupine, and dozens of kinds of smaller animals. In the Rocky Mountains are mountain goats and bighorn sheep, grizzly bears and panthers. Coyotes are common in the prairies. Most North American birds are common, including the famous Canada goose and many other kinds of geese and ducks; Canada may be the last stronghold of the increasingly rare golden and bald eagles.

All the way across Arctic Canada are the savage, dangerous polar bears. They ramble across the ice from one island to another, or swim long distances from ice floe to ice floe or from island to mainland. Their hunting is largely for seals, and it keeps them close to icy water the year around. Here, too, and across the tundras, is the little arctic fox—millions of him—white in winter and brown in summer.

On the northeast mainland of the Northwest Territories and on some of the islands to the north live the musk oxen—big, shaggy animals that survived the Ice Age. Their bodies are covered with warm, woolly blankets under coats of thick, long hair; their food is the lichens and mosses of the tundra. When threatened by an enemy, the males form a circle with the females and young inside, and present a solid wall of sturdy, sharp-horned heads against attack.

There are many other interesting members of tundra wildlife—the great snowy owl, the ptarmigan, the gulls, the Arctic tern that flies 11,000 miles to the Antarctic each fall and back again in the spring. The lemming is a small rodent. Millions of them assemble periodically on the tundra and move across the land, and drown when they swim into the ocean or other body of water too large for them to cross. Caribou, the American reindeer, also move by the thousand across the tundras, going north in search of food in spring and coming back to the forests in the fall.

In Canadian waters, walruses and seals of several kinds live all the way across the north and are the mainstay of life for the Eskimos. Whales and porpoises are common; terror among them is the savage killer whale, 30 feet long and weighing 40 tons, that will slash into any moving thing he meets. Fish are abundant, from the cod of Newfoundland to the salmon of British Columbia. And world-famous are the great colonies of gannets, puffins, murres, gulls, and other sea birds that cling to such rocky nesting grounds as Bonaventure Island, off the Gaspé Peninsula, and all the way north along the Labrador coast.

Canadian plants, too, include some of the most unusual in the world. The tundras are clothed by great masses of moss and lichens, brilliant in spring and fall with gaudy seasonal colorings. A great variety of flowering plants, too, grow on the tundra, blooming and producing seeds in the few weeks free of frost. Near the tree line, tiny, dwarfed spruce trees grow in little sheltered hollows that reach into the tundra from the forest. Contrasting with these tiny specimens are the gigantic Sitka spruce and Douglas fir of the British Columbia coastal rain forest; trees have been cut here that were more than 400 feet tall, the world's largest.

Enchantment of the Far North

High mountains and deep oceans, rivers and lakes and bays, forests and tundra and polar ice—these hold the special enchantment of the North. Find it in picturesque rapids and water-falls along almost any stream, and often, as along the Labrador coast, in deep gorges where water roars downward into the ocean. Find it in a quiet lake, river-joined to some far-flung settlement, where a steamboat moves through blue summer water. Find it in a successful walrus hunt, as the smiling black-eyed Eskimos bring in the hide and flesh and fat and bone that are the most important materials of their lives.

This is the land of the "midnight sun," itself an enchantment. North of the Arctic Circle, for an increasing number of summer days and nights as you go farther north, the sun never sets. All through the day and night, it moves low along the horizon, seemingly having just risen. At the opposite side of the year, in winter, there are days when it does not come up at all, and the arctic world is sunless.

This, too, is the land where the "northern lights" are born—the Aurora Borealis—and here they are at their finest. Great bands of color, yellow, blue, green, and red, sweep across the sky; filmy curtains, changing swiftly in color and form, hang between sky and earth.

Main Street Enchantment

From one end to the other of "Main Street," there is enchantment; to be in the midst of it, travel the Trans-Canada Highway. Start at St. John's, Newfoundland, where the highway starts, and see the fishing boats, with their catch; see Signal Hill, overlooking the beautiful harbor among rocky hills, where the world's first trans-ocean wireless message came to Marconi in 1901. Here, in August, is held St. John's Regatta, oldest sports event in North America. Follow the highway through picturesque towns and lovely ocean scenery, past Corner Brook's huge log rafts, to the tip of the island, and ferry across to Nova Scotia.

Here, in "New Scotland," are Scotch background and color; plaids and kilts and bagpipes are much in evidence, especially at the Highland

Games. Headliners among Canada's many folk festivals, these are cele-
brations with Scotch music, dancing and competitive games; there are,
every year, the Gathering of the Clans at Pugwash, the Highland Games
at Antigonish, and the Gaelic Mod at St. Ann's.

From New Brunswick, a side trip permits a visit to Prince Edward
Island's fine beaches, gardens and farms. Another to the north skirts
the Gaspé Peninsula, famed beauty spot of ocean and beach and rugged
headland; a trip by boat reaches Bonaventure Island and the fabulous
bird colonies there. Through New Brunswick the highway follows the
scenic St. John River which, near Saint John at its mouth, has the
famous "Reversing Falls"; water rushes down through a gorge to the
sea, then back again as the tide comes in.

River Cities

The picturesque St. Lawrence Valley is strongly French, capped by
the old French stronghold, the City of Quebec. Quebec is built on two
levels, Upper Town and Lower Town; Lower Town nestles against
the base of a giant stone promontory, "The Rock," while Upper Town
rides its crest. The two are connected by narrow, steep streets and
stairways. Streets are lined with French shops and stores and homes;
there are many beautiful old churches. The old Citadel stands in
Upper Town at the very edge of the promontory; back from it are the
Plains of Abraham, where the French and English fought their last
battle for New France.

Downriver from Quebec, on the north side of the river, there are
many beautiful and interesting places that tourists and vacationers like
to visit—places along the Saguenay River; Montmorency Falls on the
Montmorency River; Ste. Anne de Beaupre, shrine that has been the
goal of pilgrimages since 1658; and Isle d'Orleans, where old French
ways and customs are the way of life.

Montreal, Canada's largest city, is on a big island in the St. Lawrence,
at the mouth of the Ottawa. Here, again, is a store of historical land-
marks, as well as the excitement of the great harbor and the modern
wonders of a skyscraper city. Upriver are the fascinating new locks
and dams of the St. Lawrence Seaway and the world's ships moving

through it.

Ottawa, capital city of Canada, lies up the Ottawa River, her promontory setting dominated by the Parliament Buildings. From their tallest, Peace Tower, there is a wonderful view of river and city; and in front of the Tower, each day in summer, occurs the colorful Changing of the Guard.

From all three of these cities, many routes lead into the vast lake and forest playgrounds to the north of them. All three cities are centers of winter sports fun, climaxing each year in gay winter carnivals.

Niagara Falls

One of the great wonders of the world, Niagara Falls are part of the narrow channel that drains water from Lake Erie into Lake Ontario; over them thunders most of the water that drains down from the Great Lakes. The falls are partly in the United States, partly in Canada, and can be viewed from both countries. Walkways on riverbanks and several islands provide good spots from which to see them, and a steamboat, *Maid of the Mist,* takes visitors upriver to the foot of the falls.

Big Lakes

It is easy to imagine that enchantment lies along the borders of the Great Lakes, in such regions as Georgian Bay, with its thousands of islands and inlets; summer visitors come for fishing, swimming, boating, and sunshine. At Sault Ste. Marie there is, again, the interest of big-ship travel through locks around the rapids; and from there west to Port Arthur and Fort William is a hard-won section of highway through hard rock and forest, skirting the northern edge of Lake Superior—an interesting glimpse of the Ontario frontier.

Traveling the Trans-Canada Highway, you see the Lake of the Woods country, a region of big lakes and islands and bigger fishing, where giant muskies are the storied catch. Still farther west are Manitoba's big lakes, headed by Lake Winnipeg. These are largely wilderness lakes except for a few small settlements where roads and airlines have become established.

The Calgary Stampede

West of Winnipeg, the enchantment of "great open spaces" is that of the prairies—the vast grain fields, the big cattle ranches. Early summer brings a series of local rodeos in preparation for the world-famous king-size annual, the Calgary Stampede; the usual calf-roping and bronco-riding are climaxed by earth-shaking chuckwagon races, resembling Roman chariot races in their noise and confusion.

Mountain and Ocean

The Trans-Canada Highway travels through magnificent scenery in British Columbia's Selkirk and Columbia Mountains and follows the beautiful Fraser River down to Vancouver—Canada's queen of the Pacific. At the foot of snow-capped mountains and almost surrounded by the waters of ocean bay and river, Vancouver is one of the most beautiful cities in the world.

Across the strait on Vancouver Island is another beautiful city, Victoria, capital of British Columbia; Parliament Buildings and the magnificent old Empress Hotel have a setting of colorful gardens and parks. In Thunderbird Park is an interesting collection of totem poles and other art of the coastal Indians. Victoria has long been famous for the "Tallyho," an open sightseers' bus pulled by horses; there are several hundred in the city, each equipped with bright red blankets to keep visitors warm on a chilly day.

Vancouver Island reaches north from Victoria, a submerged mountain range with mountain peaks and sparkling lakes as well as many inlets and offshore islands all along its borders. Many resort and residence areas make use of its wonderful, year-round recreation opportunities.

From either Victoria or Vancouver, visitors can ride excursion boats. Some of these tour the waters around the two cities and the island. Others go farther north to thread the fjord-like passages between islands and into inlets, where mountains rise sheer from the water, and fishing and sight-seeing are the finest in a lifetime.

Things to think about

Some of the most famous playgrounds of North America are in Canada—can you name four of the most important ones?

What early peoples of Canada contribute to present-day entertainment of visitors?

Tell a story of the wild life of North America and its retreat to the wilderness of Canada.

What Old World enchantment is found in the eastern part of Canada?

Instant facts

Land area, 3,560,238 square miles

Fresh water area, 291,571 square miles

Total area of Canada, 3,851,809 square miles

Population 1871 (first national census)
    3,689,257

Population 1961 (Dominion Bureau of Statistics)
    18,238,247

1534 Jacques Cartier claimed the land for the King of France

1603 Champlain landed in Canada

1610-11 Hudson Bay explored by Hudson

1670 Hudson's Bay Company granted a charter

1755 The last intercolonial war begins between France and Great Britain

1759 French are defeated by the British on Plains of Abraham, Quebec

1763 Treaty of Paris: French lands in Canada are ceded to British

1793 Mackenzie crossed Rockies to reach the Pacific

1825 Lachine Canal opened

1833 First Canadian steamer, "Royal William" crossed the Atlantic

1881 Transcontinental railway completed

1959 St. Lawrence Waterway opened

Index

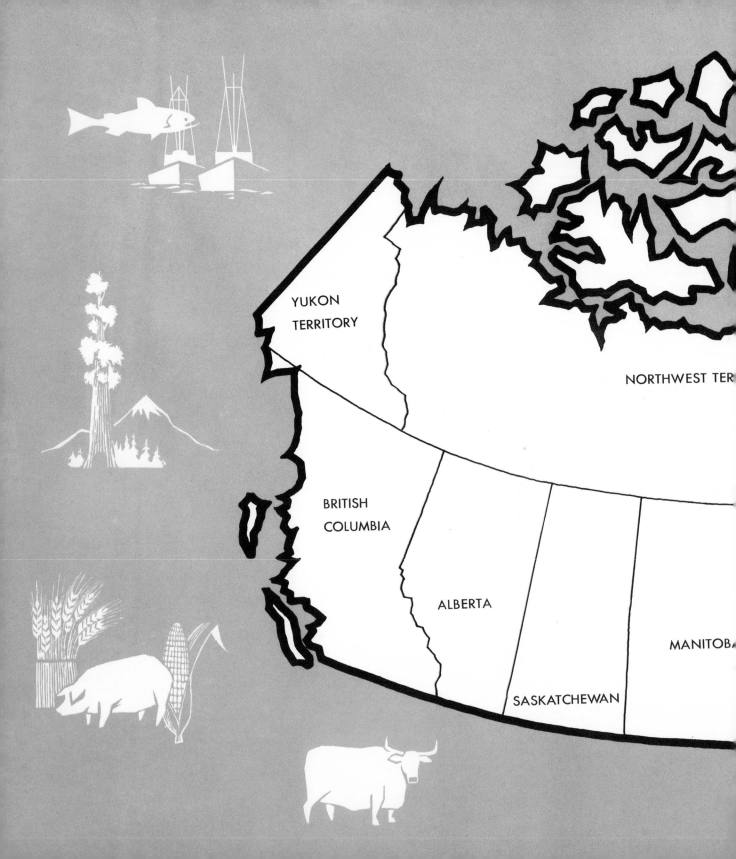

YUKON
TERRITORY

NORTHWEST TER

BRITISH
COLUMBIA

ALBERTA

SASKATCHEWAN

MANITOB

ORIES

HUDSON
BAY

ONTARIO

QUEBEC

NEWFOUNDLAND

GULF OF ST. LAWRENCE

P. E. I.

NEW
BRUNSWICK

NOVA SCOTIA